THE POWER WITHIN YOU

PAILA RAVI SANKAR

Made with ♥ on the Notion Press Platform
www.notionpress.com

To My mother

To My Friends

"The best way to live with honor in this world is to act as you really are, and if you could think about it, you would see that every human virtue is driven by that act.--Socrates"

Contents

Prologue

Hello! I'm Ravi Sankar, and I'm truly excited to invite you on this transformative journey to discover the power within you. As I write these words, I feel a deep sense of gratitude for the opportunity to walk this path alongside you. This book is about unlocking the true potential within yourself through self-compassion, gratitude, and a more loving, confident relationship with who you are.

In these pages, we'll explore powerful tools and practices that can help you reconnect with your authentic self and cultivate lasting peace and happiness. The journey is broken down into two main subtopics for each chapter, each designed to guide you toward deeper self-awareness and positive change:

Subtopic 1: In this section, we'll dive into a specific theme, exploring it from both a conceptual and practical standpoint. You'll gain insights into how these concepts can help you change the way you approach life, especially the moments when you tend to be hard on yourself. This is where you'll discover practical strategies to promote kindness, understanding, and self-compassion in your everyday life.

Subtopic 2: In this section, you'll engage in a simple but powerful journaling practice. Each chapter will offer a prompt or exercise that invites you to reflect, affirm, and express gratitude. This practice is designed to deepen your connection with yourself and strengthen your emotional resilience.

For the journaling exercises, you can choose the method that feels most comfortable to you:

Pen and Paper: If you enjoy the tactile experience of writing by hand, you can use a notebook to record your thoughts, affirmations, and reflections each day. Writing with a pen offers a personal touch that helps solidify your connection to your intentions and emotions.

Digital Journaling: Alternatively, if you prefer digital tools, you can use any app or software that helps you stay organized and motivated. The key is to create a space where you can freely express yourself.

No matter how you choose to journal, the goal is to create a practice that resonates with you—one that brings you back to your center and helps you grow in self-love and understanding.

I'm so grateful to have you here, and I can't wait for you to embark on this journey of self-discovery. Let's dive in and start exploring the incredible power within you.

ONE

Unlock Your Potential

Now is the time to let go of any doubts you have about yourself and what you can do. It's not always easy, I know, but let's try. Don't think about forever—just focus on right now. In this moment, tell yourself: I can do this. I can love myself. I can be someone I love unconditionally.

We spend so much energy loving others—let's promise to love ourselves too. Starting today, you'll work on changing the way you think and focusing on what's good for you.

Instead of saying, This won't work for me or I'm not sure I can do this, say, I'm excited to start my self-love journey and do my best for myself.

When you start something new, doubt often sneaks in. But think about how you'd support a friend if they were trying something good for themselves—you'd cheer them on, right? You need to do the same for yourself. You can do this. You can love yourself. You have what it takes.

I know you do. I've been through this journey myself, and I promise you're capable.

Don't let self-doubt stop you. You can take its power away by changing how you talk to yourself.

Here are some affirmations to help you:

I am my best source of inspiration.

I can overcome any challenge.

I respect myself and my goals.

I can achieve what I set my mind to.

I am strong and full of belief in myself.

I trust in my abilities.

I am on the path to great things.

I have amazing potential.

I shape my own future.

I am grateful for my possibilities.

Prompt:

Imagine what your ideal relationship with yourself would look like. How would you feel? Write about it as if it's already true.

Think about feeling confident, peaceful, and connected with yourself. Be realistic but positive—describe it in detail, as if you're already living it. Let your thoughts flow naturally.

Example:

I feel happy with who I am. I'm at peace with myself and speak to myself with kindness. I feel like my own best friend, and I'm filled with gratitude for reaching this point. Loving myself feels incredible, and I'm so thankful for this journey. I am proud of who I've become.

TWO

FAREWELL TO COMPARISON

This topic can be tricky. When we see people around us who seem successful or happy, we might want to be like them. It could be in how they look, act, work, shop, speak, or something else.

This often leads to comparing ourselves to them, which can make us feel like we're not good enough. It also makes them seem perfect, but no one is perfect. They might even be comparing themselves to others—or to you, if they know you.

There's a healthier way to handle this. We can't avoid seeing examples of success around us, and that's a good thing! But we should choose to see it with kindness towards ourselves, not with negativity. When you notice someone awesome, take inspiration from them. Don't think of it as a competition or feel like you're less than them. Instead, make it about learning.

For example, if someone dresses well, compliment them and learn from their style. If someone has a great voice, don't criticize your own. Instead, notice what you like about their voice and think about how you can improve yours.

Sometimes, it's enough to just appreciate others without comparing yourself. If you do think of yourself, do it in a positive way. We are all unique, yet we share similarities. Comparison isn't helpful—what matters is celebrating our uniqueness and being part of this world together.

Now, let's focus on positive affirmations:

Affirmations for Confidence

I am happy with my life and at peace in my mind and heart.

I am kind to myself as I grow.

I am grateful for my unique qualities.

I celebrate the success of others.

I support my friends and loved ones who are doing well.

I let go of jealousy—it has no place in my life.

I stop comparing myself to others.

I embrace my journey because it's uniquely mine.

I am beautiful, inside and out.

I am important.

Prompt for Today

Write about what makes you unique and the people who have inspired you.

Think about how there's no one exactly like you. You share similarities with others, but you're one of a kind. Celebrate yourself and those who've guided or inspired you.

Example:

"I am grateful for my quirks and qualities. There's only one me with this unique mix of traits, and I'm happy to be myself. Many people have inspired me, and I can see parts of their influence in who I am. I'm thankful for all of them."

THREE

ART OF MIND CONTROL

The mind is a powerful tool, one that can shape our reality, influence our emotions, and determine our actions. Often, we feel as though we are at the mercy of our thoughts—stressed, overwhelmed, or lost in negative patterns. But what if we could take control of our minds, rather than letting them control us?

The art of mind control is not about forcing thoughts or emotions into submission. It's about mastering the ability to guide your mind, redirecting it with intention and awareness. It's about recognizing that you have the power to shift your focus, your thoughts, and your mindset at any moment.

When you learn to control your mind, you open up the possibility for a life filled with clarity, purpose, and peace. You become the creator of your own reality, able to navigate life's challenges with resilience and confidence.

Here's how to practice the art of mind control:

Awareness is the first step: The moment you become aware of your thoughts, you gain power over them. Observe your thinking patterns without judgment. Are you engaging in negative self-talk or getting stuck in worries? Simply noticing these thoughts gives you the freedom to change them.

Challenge your thoughts: Don't accept every thought as truth. When negative or limiting thoughts arise, ask yourself: "Is this thought helpful?" "Is this based on facts?" Challenge your assumptions and replace them with more empowering beliefs.

Focus on the present: The mind loves to wander—into the past or future. But the present moment is where your power lies. Practice mindfulness by bringing your attention back to the here and now. This will help reduce anxiety and keep your mind from spiraling out of control.

Reframe negative thoughts: Instead of focusing on the problem, focus on the solution. If you find yourself overwhelmed by a challenge, reframe your thinking: "What can I learn from this? How can I use this to grow?" Shifting your mindset opens up new possibilities and fosters resilience.

Visualize positive outcomes: Visualization is a powerful tool for controlling your mind. By picturing positive scenarios and imagining your goals being achieved, you can reprogram your subconscious mind to believe in your success. Your mind is most receptive to positive imagery when it's calm.

Practice gratitude: Gratitude brings your attention back to what's good and positive in your life. When you focus on what you have, rather than what you lack, you retrain your mind to see opportunities, not obstacles. Gratitude is a mental practice that strengthens emotional resilience.

Cultivate mental discipline: Mind control requires practice. Just like physical exercise, strengthening the mind takes time and discipline. Build mental resilience through consistent practices such as meditation, deep breathing, journaling, and affirmations. The more you exercise control over your thoughts, the stronger you become.

Affirmations for mastering the art of mind control:

I am in control of my thoughts, and I choose peace over chaos.

My mind is a tool that I use to create the life I desire.

I have the power to change my thoughts and shift my mindset.

I control my emotions; they do not control me.

I choose to focus on what I can control and release what I cannot.

Every day, I become more aware of my thinking patterns.

I have the strength to challenge negative thoughts and replace them with positive beliefs.

My mind is calm, focused, and disciplined.

I am the master of my thoughts and emotions.

I trust in my ability to shape my own reality through the power of my mind.

Prompt: Be thankful for the ability to control your mind.

Your mind is a tool, a powerful ally in creating the life you want. By mastering it, you become the architect of your reality, able to transform challenges into opportunities and negative emotions into strengths. Mind control isn't about suppressing your thoughts—it's about learning to direct them toward what serves you best. Be thankful for this ability, for it's through your mind that you have the power to shape every aspect of your life.

Example:

I'm grateful for my ability to control my mind. When my thoughts become overwhelming or negative, I remember that I have the power to shift them. I choose to focus on what brings me peace and clarity. My mind is my ally, and I am thankful for the strength it gives me to navigate life's challenges.

FOUR

Accept and Honor Your Emotions

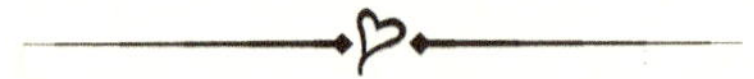

It's important to allow ourselves to feel whatever emotions come up and be okay with the range of feelings we experience. I believe it's essential to embrace all the emotions life brings.

Feeling sadness is especially important. But I also understand how hard it is to deal with depression and anxiety, where you may feel things without any clear reason and wish you didn't feel that way. This isn't about those experiences.

This session is about the emotions we need to feel and accept.

It's okay to feel nervous when sharing your opinions—it means you're stepping out of your comfort zone.

It's okay to feel afraid when making a big decision—it shows you're brave enough to choose what's right for you.

It's okay to feel sad when you miss someone you love—it means they matter to you and remind you of happy moments together.

It's okay to feel angry when you're mistreated—it shows you respect yourself.

It's okay to feel guilty when you make a mistake—it means you care about your values.

It's okay to feel emotions—they remind you that you're alive.

You don't need to pretend to be okay when you're not. There is strength in being honest with yourself. Staying connected to your emotions helps you avoid unnecessary stress and the need to escape them. Life is about these feelings, and it's best to live them fully.

Now, let's focus on affirmations:

I have the right to feel this way.

The best gift I can give myself and others is understanding what I need in this moment. The inner work I do helps those around me, too.

I have the freedom to choose how I color my emotional world.

I can handle my emotions with ease.

It's okay for me to experience and embrace my feelings.

My feelings are important and valid.

I am doing my best each day.

I am truthful with myself.

I prioritize my emotions and take care of my well-being.

I respect my feelings and value my life.

Prompt: Be thankful for the ability to experience life through your emotions.

Imagine how dull life would be if everything was the same and without change. Our emotions remind us that we are alive and can truly experience life. It's a gift. Let's be thankful for the ability to feel.

Example:

I'm thankful for all the emotions I can feel. They make my life interesting and full. They help me feel alive and aware of the present moment. My emotions show me what things really mean to me and how they fit into my life. I'm grateful to be able to experience this world.

FIVE

Convert Strees into Smile

Stress is a part of life, but it doesn't have to define how we experience it. Life's demands, challenges, and surprises can often feel overwhelming, but in these moments, we have a powerful choice: to convert our stress into something positive. We can turn stress into a smile, not by ignoring it or pretending it's not there, but by shifting our perspective and response.

When you feel stressed, remember that your emotions are signals—signals that show you care, that you're engaged, and that you're working through something meaningful. The key is not to let stress control you but to learn how to manage it in ways that benefit you.

Here's how to convert stress into a smile:

Acknowledge your stress: Recognizing that you're stressed is the first step. It's okay to feel it; don't fight it. Understanding it is the path to transforming it.

Take a deep breath: Deep breathing activates your parasympathetic nervous system and helps calm the body's stress response. Just a few moments of mindful breathing can create space between the stress and your reaction.

Find the humor: Laughter has incredible healing power. Sometimes, stepping back and finding the humor in a stressful situation can instantly lighten the mood. Life doesn't have to be taken so seriously.

Shift your perspective: Instead of focusing on the overwhelming parts of your stress, look at what you can learn from the situation. Stress can teach you valuable lessons about yourself, your limits, and what you truly value.

Practice gratitude: When we are stressed, it's easy to focus on what's going wrong. Shift your attention to what's going right. Gratitude has the power to shift our mindset and instantly change our emotional state.

Smile anyway: Even if it feels unnatural, try smiling. The physical act of smiling can trick your brain into thinking you're happier, and in turn, it can actually help reduce stress hormones.

Affirmations to turn stress into smile:

I acknowledge my stress, but I choose to manage it with grace.

I am capable of transforming my stress into strength.

Every challenge I face is an opportunity to grow.

I can handle whatever comes my way with a calm and positive mindset.

I choose to find peace, even in stressful moments.

My smile is a reminder that I have control over my response.

I am resilient, and I can turn stress into motivation.

I am grateful for the opportunity to learn and grow through stress.

I am in control of my emotions and reactions.

I choose to smile because I know stress is temporary, and I am capable.

Prompt: Be thankful for your ability to convert stress into strength and joy.

Stress is inevitable, but how we respond to it is a gift. We can choose to face it with a positive mindset, finding moments of laughter, calm, and strength within the pressure. It's not about removing stress from our lives—it's about learning how to navigate it in a way that empowers us. Each time we choose to smile in the face of stress, we reinforce our resilience and embrace the beauty of life's ups and downs.

Example:

I'm thankful for my ability to transform stress into a smile. Every time I face a challenge, I grow stronger and more resilient. I choose to see the humor and opportunity in stressful moments, knowing that my smile is a reminder of my strength. I am grateful for the balance I create in my life by turning stress into something positive.

SIX

ART OF SELF MANAGEMENT

Self-management is the foundation of personal success and well-being. It is the ability to take control of your life, making deliberate choices about how you use your time, energy, and resources. Life is full of distractions, obligations, and challenges, but those who master the art of self-management can navigate them with intention, clarity, and balance. It's not about being perfect or having everything under control all the time; it's about being conscious of your decisions and aligning them with your values and goals.

When you practice self-management, you gain the freedom to create a life that aligns with your deepest desires. You develop habits and strategies that support your growth, well-being, and productivity, without sacrificing your peace of mind. It's about learning how to prioritize what matters most and letting go of what no longer serves you.

Here's how to practice the art of self-management:

Set clear goals and intentions: Start by defining what you want to achieve in both the short term and long term. Clear goals give you direction and focus. Break them down into actionable steps so that you can make progress every day. Setting intentions ensures that you align your actions with your values.

Prioritize what matters: Time is your most precious resource, so use it wisely. Identify your top priorities—whether it's work, family, health, or personal growth—and make sure they receive the attention they deserve. Let go of the things that drain your energy or distract you from your goals.

Create routines that work for you: Consistency is key to self-management. Develop routines that promote productivity and well-being. This could include a morning ritual to start your day with intention, time-blocking for focused work, or evening practices that help you unwind and prepare for rest. Routines create structure and make it easier to manage your time and energy.

Practice time management: Time is finite, and effective self-management requires mastering time management skills. Use techniques like the Pomodoro method, time-blocking, or to-do lists to stay organized. Avoid multitasking, which can reduce productivity and increase stress. Focus on one task at a time, and give it your full attention.

Learn to say no: Part of self-management is setting boundaries. Recognize that you cannot do everything, and that's okay. Learn to say no to things that don't align with your priorities or that drain your energy. Saying no is a powerful act of self-respect and a way to protect your time and resources.

Cultivate self-discipline: Self-discipline is the ability to do what needs to be done, even when you don't feel like it. It's about staying committed to your goals and following through, even in the face of challenges. Practice small acts of self-discipline each day, whether it's sticking to a workout routine, finishing a task on time, or resisting distractions.

Manage your emotions: Effective self-management involves emotional awareness and regulation. Recognize how your emotions influence your decisions and actions. Practice mindfulness to stay grounded and calm. When you manage your emotions, you make better choices and reduce stress.

Embrace self-care: Self-management is not just about work and productivity; it's also about taking care of your mind, body, and spirit. Make time for self-care practices that nourish you, whether it's exercise, meditation, creative hobbies, or social connection. When you care for yourself, you have the energy and focus to manage all other aspects of your life.

Reflect and adjust: Regular reflection is key to continuous improvement. At the end of each day or week, take a moment to evaluate your progress. What went well? What could be improved? Adjust your strategies as needed, and celebrate your wins. This helps you stay on track and make better decisions moving forward.

Affirmations for mastering the art of self-management:

I am in control of my time and energy.

I make intentional choices that align with my values and goals.

I prioritize what matters most and let go of distractions.

I am disciplined and focused, even in the face of challenges.

I create routines that support my productivity and well-being.

I manage my time effectively and stay organized.

I honor my boundaries and say no when needed.

I am committed to my personal growth and success.

I take care of my mind, body, and spirit.

I reflect on my progress and make adjustments to stay aligned with my goals.

Prompt: Be thankful for your ability to manage yourself.

Self-management is a skill that empowers you to create a balanced, fulfilling life. By managing your time, energy, and emotions, you can achieve your goals without sacrificing your well-being. It's a practice of self-respect and personal growth—learning to navigate life with purpose, clarity, and intention. Be grateful for the ability to manage yourself, for it gives you the freedom to design your life in a way that serves your highest potential.

Example:

I'm thankful for my ability to manage myself. Every choice I make brings me closer to my goals, and every step I take is a reflection of my values. I honor my time, my energy, and my emotions, and I use them wisely. I am grateful for the clarity and focus that self-management brings into my life, allowing me to create balance and live with purpose.

SEVEN

OVERCOMING FEAR

Fear is a natural part of life, but it doesn't have to hold us back. It's a protective mechanism, alerting us to potential danger, but it can also become a barrier that prevents us from pursuing our dreams and living our fullest life. The art of overcoming fear is not about eliminating it entirely, but about learning to move forward despite it.

Fear can show up in many forms: fear of failure, fear of the unknown, fear of rejection, or fear of change. It can paralyze us, keeping us stuck in a cycle of hesitation and self-doubt. But when we learn to acknowledge and face our fears, we gain the power to transform them into a source of strength, motivation, and growth.

Overcoming fear is a practice—a process of gradually taking control of the way we respond to fear. Instead of allowing fear to dictate our actions, we can use it as a signal to grow, to step outside our comfort zones, and to embrace new opportunities.

Here's how to overcome fear:

Acknowledge your fear: The first step in overcoming fear is to acknowledge it without judgment. Fear often thrives in the darkness of denial, so by recognizing it and naming it, you take away its power. Ask yourself: What exactly am I afraid of? Understanding the root of your fear helps you face it more effectively.

Shift your perspective: Fear is often based on imagined outcomes or worst-case scenarios. Challenge these thoughts. Ask yourself: "What's the most likely outcome?" "What can I learn from this situation, regardless of the result?" Shifting your perspective from fear of failure to opportunity for growth can help you view fear as a tool for progress, rather than an obstacle.

Take small steps: Overcoming fear is rarely about taking giant leaps all at once. Instead, break down your goals or challenges into small, manageable steps. Every small action you take in the face of fear builds confidence and reduces its power over time. The more you expose yourself to what frightens you in manageable doses, the less control fear will have over you.

Visualize success: Visualization is a powerful tool for overcoming fear. Imagine yourself succeeding in the situation that frightens you. Picture yourself navigating it with calm and confidence. The more vividly you can see yourself succeeding, the more you program your mind to expect positive outcomes rather than catastrophic ones.

Practice mindfulness and breathing: Fear often triggers a fight-or-flight response, which can cause physical tension and anxiety. Practice deep breathing or mindfulness techniques to calm your body and mind. When you're present in the moment, your fear loses its hold over you. Breathing deeply or focusing on your senses helps you center yourself and reduces the intensity of fear.

Embrace discomfort: Fear often arises when we step outside our comfort zones. Recognize that discomfort is a natural part of growth. Instead of avoiding discomfort, lean into it. The more you embrace discomfort, the more resilient you become. Understand that growth happens when you push through the fear and expand your boundaries.

Reframe failure: Fear of failure is one of the most common fears we face. But failure is not the end—it's a part of the journey toward success. When you reframe failure as feedback, you allow yourself to try again with more wisdom and experience. Fear of failure loses its grip when you understand that failure is not something to be afraid of, but something to learn from.

Build a support system: Fear can feel isolating, but you don't have to face it alone. Surround yourself with people who encourage and support you. Having a support system can provide comfort, advice, and a sense of solidarity as you navigate your fears. Sharing your fears with others helps you feel less alone and more empowered.

Celebrate your bravery: Every time you face your fear, no matter how small the step, celebrate your courage. Acknowledge your bravery and recognize your progress. The more you celebrate, the more you reinforce your ability to overcome fear in the future. Positive reinforcement builds confidence and strengthens your resolve.

Affirmations for overcoming fear:

I acknowledge my fear, but I do not let it control me.

Fear is a signal for me to grow, not something to avoid.

I am stronger than my fear, and I can face any challenge.

Every step I take in the face of fear makes me braver and more confident.

I trust myself to handle whatever comes my way.

I choose courage over comfort.

I learn and grow from every experience, even if it includes failure.

I am capable of achieving my goals, no matter how big the fear.

I embrace discomfort because it leads to growth.

Fear is temporary, but the strength I gain from overcoming it lasts forever.

Prompt: Be thankful for your ability to overcome fear.

Fear is a natural part of life, but it doesn't have to control us. Every time you face your fear and choose to take action, you grow stronger and more resilient. You prove to yourself that you are capable of navigating uncertainty, overcoming challenges, and achieving greatness. Fear is not the enemy; it is the invitation to evolve. Be thankful for the opportunity to conquer your fears, for it is through this process that you unlock your true potential.

Example:
I'm thankful for my ability to overcome fear. Every time I face a fear, I learn something new about myself. I grow stronger, braver, and more confident. I trust that fear is a guide, not a roadblock. It's through overcoming fear that I discover my true strength and resilience. I am grateful for the courage within me to step into the unknown and embrace the opportunities that await.

EIGHT

POWER OF HABITS

Habits are the invisible forces that shape our lives. They are the small, repetitive actions we take each day, often without thinking, that collectively determine our success, well-being, and happiness. Whether they are positive or negative, our habits have a profound impact on our future. The power of habits lies in their ability to create momentum in our lives, to help us achieve our goals, and to shape our reality, one small action at a time.

Good habits are the foundation of personal growth, productivity, and health. When we consciously choose the habits that serve our highest potential, we build a life that reflects our values and desires. The beauty of habits is that, over time, they become second nature, creating a structure that supports us even when our motivation fluctuates.

The art of mastering habits is understanding that it's not about making drastic changes all at once, but about making small, sustainable shifts that compound over time. With consistency and patience, we can transform our daily actions and create the life we want.

Here's how to harness the power of habits:

Start small and be consistent: The key to building lasting habits is starting small. Trying to make drastic changes can overwhelm you and lead to burnout. Instead, choose one small habit you want to develop, and commit to it consistently. Whether it's drinking more water, exercising for 10 minutes a day, or writing in a journal, consistency is what makes habits stick.

Focus on the process, not the outcome: It's easy to get discouraged when we only focus on the end result. Instead, shift your attention to the process itself. Enjoy the act of doing, not just the goal you're working toward. When you focus on the small wins and progress, you build a positive feedback loop that motivates you to keep going.

Create triggers for your habits: Every habit needs a cue to remind you to take action. Set up external triggers—like placing your workout clothes next to your bed or putting your journal on your desk—to prompt the behavior. These triggers act as reminders and make it easier to follow through with your habits.

Track your progress: Tracking your habits helps you stay accountable and see how far you've come. Whether you use a habit tracker app, a calendar, or a journal, tracking helps you stay motivated and reinforces your commitment to your goals. Celebrate each small milestone as it builds momentum.

Replace bad habits with good ones: Instead of trying to eliminate bad habits directly, replace them with positive ones. For example, if you tend to snack on unhealthy foods when stressed, replace the habit with a healthier alternative, like drinking a cup of tea or going for a walk. Over time, the new habit will naturally replace the old one.

Make it easy and enjoyable: The more enjoyable and easy you make a habit, the more likely you are to stick with it. Find ways to make the process fun and rewarding. For example, if you're trying to develop a reading habit, choose books that you're genuinely excited about, or set up a cozy reading space that you love spending time in.

Be patient and kind to yourself: Building new habits takes time. It's normal to experience setbacks or slip-ups along the way. The key is to stay patient and not to judge yourself too harshly. Every day is a new opportunity to get back on track. Remember, it's the consistency over time that makes the biggest difference.

Celebrate your successes: Every time you stick to your habit, take a moment to celebrate your success, no matter how small. Positive reinforcement helps strengthen the habit loop and motivates you to keep going. Celebrate the process, the progress, and the person you're becoming.

Reflect and adjust: Periodically take time to reflect on your habits. Are they still serving your goals? Do you need to adjust or add new habits? Self-reflection helps you stay aligned with your intentions and ensures that your habits continue to support your growth and well-being.

Affirmations for harnessing the power of habits:

I am in control of my habits, and I choose habits that serve my growth.

I take small, consistent actions every day that move me closer to my goals.

I focus on the process, not just the outcome, and enjoy the journey.

My positive habits create momentum in my life and help me achieve my dreams.

Every day, I grow stronger and more disciplined in my habits.

I am patient with myself, knowing that change takes time.

I replace bad habits with habits that support my health, happiness, and success.

I celebrate every small win along the way.

I am becoming the best version of myself through my daily habits.

The habits I cultivate today shape the life I create tomorrow.

Prompt: Be thankful for the power of your habits.

Our habits are the silent architects of our lives, shaping our future one small action at a time. When we choose our habits consciously, we create a life that aligns with our values, desires, and goals. Every positive habit you create brings you closer to the life you envision. Be thankful for the power of habits, for they hold the key to unlocking your potential and shaping your destiny.

Example:
I'm grateful for the power of my habits. Every day, the small actions I take compound to create a life that reflects my deepest values and aspirations. I am thankful for the consistency that helps me stay on track, and for the process of growth that habits bring. With every positive habit I build, I am becoming the best version of myself.

NINE

LISTEN TO YOUR INTUITION

Intuition is often described as a quiet inner voice, a feeling, or a sense of knowing that guides us, even when logic or reasoning can't provide clear answers. It's that gut feeling you get when something doesn't feel right or when you know you should take a certain path, even though you don't have all the details. Your intuition is a powerful tool—a deep wisdom within you that connects you to your inner truth and helps you navigate life with clarity and confidence.

Listening to your intuition is about trusting yourself and honoring the quiet guidance that comes from within. It's not always easy to hear, especially in a world full of distractions and external opinions. But when you learn to tune in, you tap into a wellspring of insight that can lead you toward the right decisions, meaningful connections, and authentic experiences.

The art of listening to your intuition requires slowing down, quieting the noise, and learning to distinguish between the voices of fear, doubt, and true inner wisdom. It's about cultivating self-trust, being open to what arises, and following the path that feels aligned with your highest good.

Here's how to listen to your intuition:

Create space for quiet: In order to hear your intuition, you need to give yourself space to listen. This means intentionally slowing down and finding moments of quiet. Whether through meditation, journaling, or simply spending time alone in nature, quieting the external noise helps you tune into your inner voice.

Trust your gut feelings: Often, your intuition speaks through physical sensations in your body—like a gut feeling or a sense of unease. Pay attention to these sensations. If something feels off or if a particular decision feels right, honor those feelings. Trust that your body and mind are signaling something important.

Practice mindfulness: Mindfulness helps you become present and aware of your thoughts, feelings, and instincts in real-time. When you practice mindfulness, you become better at discerning the difference between fear-based reactions and true intuitive insights. Take time to check in with yourself throughout the day, asking: "How does this situation feel? Does it resonate with me?"

Let go of doubt and overthinking: Intuition often speaks softly, and doubt can easily drown it out. Overthinking, second-guessing, and seeking external validation can cloud your inner wisdom. Practice letting go of the need for certainty and trust that your intuition knows what's best for you. You don't need all the answers right now—trust the process.

Pay attention to signs and synchronicities: Sometimes, your intuition speaks through external signs—coincidences, synchronicities, or recurring patterns that point you in a certain direction. Stay open to the messages the universe is sending you. Whether it's a repeated dream, a meaningful encounter, or a sense of clarity during a quiet moment, these signs can guide you to your truth.

Develop self-trust: The more you listen to your intuition and see the positive outcomes it leads you to, the more you strengthen your self-trust. Every time you follow your inner guidance and it proves to be right, your confidence in your intuitive abilities grows. Cultivate this trust by reflecting on times when your intuition has guided you in the past.

Embrace stillness: Intuition thrives in stillness. In our fast-paced world, it's easy to overlook the subtle whispers of intuition. Set aside time each day to be still—whether through meditation, deep breathing, or simply sitting in silence. This stillness opens the space for your intuition to speak more clearly.

Let your intuition guide your decisions: The more you practice listening to your intuition, the more it becomes a trusted guide in making decisions. Instead of relying solely on logic, facts, or the opinions of others, turn inward. Ask yourself: "What feels right in my heart?" Trust that the answers are already within you, waiting to be discovered.

Be patient and compassionate with yourself: Sometimes, intuition doesn't provide immediate answers. It may be subtle, or it may take time to develop clarity. Be patient with yourself as you learn to trust your inner wisdom. Allow yourself to make mistakes along the way, knowing that each step is part of the process of deepening your connection to your intuition.

Affirmations for listening to your intuition:

I trust my intuition to guide me toward what's best for me.

I am open to the wisdom that comes from within.

I listen to my inner voice with clarity and confidence.

I trust my gut feelings and honor them as truth.

My intuition always leads me toward growth and positive change.

I am patient with myself as I learn to listen to my intuition.

I trust that the answers I seek are already within me.

I embrace the signs and synchronicities that guide me.

I release doubt and overthinking, and follow my inner wisdom.

My intuition is a powerful tool that supports me in making aligned decisions.

Prompt: Be thankful for the power of your intuition.

Your intuition is a gift—a source of inner wisdom that helps you navigate life with clarity and confidence. By learning to listen to it, you align yourself with your highest good and create a life that is authentic and fulfilling. Be grateful for the guidance your intuition offers, for it is always there to lead you toward the path that serves your greatest potential.

Example:

I'm thankful for my intuition. It is my inner compass, guiding me toward the decisions and actions that align with my truth. I trust the subtle whispers of my inner wisdom and listen to them with patience and openness. I am grateful for the clarity and insight that intuition brings into my life, helping me make decisions with confidence and peace of mind.

TEN

FILL YOUR CUP FIRST

In the hustle and bustle of everyday life, it's easy to become overwhelmed with responsibilities, obligations, and the needs of others. We often prioritize taking care of everyone and everything around us, while neglecting our own well-being. But the truth is, you can't pour from an empty cup. In order to give your best to the world, you must first take care of yourself.

"Filling your cup first" is a powerful reminder that self-care is not selfish—it's essential. When you nurture yourself, physically, emotionally, and spiritually, you recharge your energy, regain clarity, and strengthen your capacity to support others. It's like putting on your own oxygen mask before helping others in an airplane emergency; only when you're well-rested, healthy, and centered can you truly be present and effective for those around you.

Self-care is not a luxury; it's a necessity for a balanced, fulfilling life. It's about honoring your own needs, setting healthy boundaries, and making time for the things that replenish you. When you prioritize your well-being, you create a ripple effect of positivity, growth, and abundance in every area of your life.

Here's how to fill your cup first:

Prioritize self-care: Self-care is the foundation of a healthy life. It's not just about taking bubble baths or getting massages (though those things can be lovely!). It's about taking care of your physical, mental, and emotional health. Eat nourishing food, move your body, rest when needed, and make time for activities that bring you joy and relaxation. Treat your well-being as a priority, not an afterthought.

Set healthy boundaries: One of the most important ways to fill your cup is to learn to say no. You don't have to do everything for everyone. Setting boundaries protects your energy and ensures that you don't give more than you have to offer. Be clear about your limits and communicate them with kindness and respect. Remember, it's okay to say no, and it's necessary for maintaining your own balance.

Make time for yourself: Life can be busy, but it's essential to carve out time for yourself—time to recharge, reflect, and simply be. Schedule "me time" into your day or week, just as you would any important appointment. Whether it's reading a book, going for a walk, meditating, or enjoying a hobby, giving yourself time to unwind and relax helps restore your energy.

Practice mindfulness: Being present with yourself is an important way to fill your cup. Practice mindfulness by checking in with yourself regularly throughout the day. Notice how you're feeling physically and emotionally. Are you tired, stressed, or overwhelmed? Give yourself permission to pause and breathe, and take a moment to replenish your energy before moving forward.

Nourish your body: Your physical health is deeply connected to your mental and emotional well-being. Fuel your body with nutritious food, stay hydrated, and get enough sleep. Regular exercise is also a powerful way to replenish your energy and release stress. When you care for your body, it supports all other areas of your life, helping you feel more energized and vibrant.

Embrace the power of rest: Rest is often undervalued in our fast-paced world, but it's one of the most important ways to fill your cup. Adequate sleep, relaxation, and taking breaks throughout the day help your body and mind recover and recharge. Don't feel guilty for resting—when you allow yourself to rest, you're better equipped to show up fully for the things and people that matter most.

Engage in activities that bring you joy: What fills you up with energy and happiness? Is it painting, hiking, cooking, or spending time with loved ones? Make sure to prioritize activities that bring you joy and allow you to reconnect with your inner self. These moments of joy help restore your spirit and create balance in your life.

Reflect and let go: Regular self-reflection helps you check in with yourself and identify what's depleting your energy. Are there relationships, habits, or commitments that drain you? Take time to reflect on what you need to release in order to make space for self-care and growth. Letting go of what no longer serves you is an act of self-love and a way to protect your energy.

Be kind to yourself: Fill your cup with compassion. Sometimes, we're our own harshest critics, pushing ourselves too hard and not allowing ourselves the grace we deserve. Practice self-compassion by being gentle with yourself. Acknowledge your efforts and progress, even when things don't go perfectly. Treat yourself with the same love and kindness you offer to others.

Affirmations for filling your cup first:

I honor my needs and prioritize my well-being.

Taking care of myself is a priority, not a luxury.

I fill my cup first so I can show up fully for others.

I set healthy boundaries to protect my energy.

I deserve time to rest, recharge, and reflect.

My body is my temple, and I nourish it with love and care.

I embrace rest as a vital part of my self-care.

I engage in activities that bring me joy and restore my spirit.

I am kind to myself and practice self-compassion.

I let go of what drains me and make space for what nourishes me.

Prompt: Be thankful for the opportunity to fill your cup first.

By filling your cup first, you give yourself the opportunity to live from a place of abundance. When you nurture yourself, you have the energy, clarity, and strength to be there for others in meaningful ways. Remember, self-care is not selfish—it's an essential part of living a balanced, fulfilling life. Be grateful for the chance to prioritize your own needs, for it allows you to show up as the best version of yourself.

Example:

I'm thankful for the opportunity to fill my cup first. By taking care of myself, I am able to give more fully to others and show up with greater energy, clarity, and love. I honor my needs and create space for rest, reflection, and joy. I am grateful for the balance that self-care brings into my life, allowing me to nurture my well-being and support those I care about with abundance.

ELEVEN

PROGRESS, NOT PERFECTION

In a world that often celebrates perfection, it's easy to fall into the trap of thinking that if we can't do something flawlessly, then it's not worth doing at all. We put immense pressure on ourselves to get everything right, whether it's in our work, relationships, or personal growth. But the truth is, perfection is an illusion. It's an unattainable standard that only leads to frustration, burnout, and feelings of inadequacy.

The real power lies in progress. Progress is about moving forward, no matter how small the steps may be. It's about recognizing that growth is a journey, not a destination. Every day you make an effort, take a step, or learn something new, you are making progress. And that progress, over time, leads to transformation.

By focusing on progress instead of perfection, we free ourselves from unrealistic expectations and embrace the beauty of the process. We give ourselves permission to fail, learn, and improve, knowing that each experience, each challenge, and each effort is a valuable part of our growth.

Here's how to focus on progress, not perfection:

Shift your mindset: The first step is to change the way you think about success. Instead of viewing perfection as the goal, see progress as your measure of success. Ask yourself, "What did I learn today?" or "How did I grow, even in small ways?" Shifting the focus from perfection to progress allows you to celebrate every step forward, no matter how small.

Set realistic goals: Perfectionism often stems from setting impossible standards for ourselves. Instead of aiming for perfection, set achievable, realistic goals that you can work toward over time. Break larger goals into smaller, manageable steps and celebrate each milestone along the way. This approach helps you stay motivated and see the progress you're making.

Embrace mistakes as learning opportunities: Mistakes are a natural part of the learning process. Instead of viewing them as failures, embrace them as opportunities to grow. Each mistake teaches you something valuable and helps you improve. Remember, perfection is not the goal—growth and learning are.

Let go of comparison: Comparing yourself to others can create feelings of inadequacy and make you feel like you're not doing enough. Everyone's journey is unique, and focusing on your own progress will help you stay grounded. Celebrate where you are and how far you've come, rather than looking at where others are and feeling like you're falling short.

Practice self-compassion: Perfectionism can be harsh and unforgiving. Instead of being your own toughest critic, practice self-compassion. Treat yourself with kindness, patience, and understanding, just as you would treat a friend. When you're kind to yourself, you create a safe space to learn and grow without fear of judgment.

Celebrate small wins: Progress is built on small, consistent actions. Take time to celebrate the little victories along the way, whether it's completing a task, overcoming a fear, or learning something new. These small wins accumulate over time and create a sense of accomplishment and motivation to keep moving forward.

Be patient with the process: Growth takes time. Be patient with yourself as you navigate the ups and downs of your journey. Perfection is a myth; progress is the real achievement. Trust that every effort you make is moving you closer to where you want to be, even if it doesn't look perfect along the way.

Focus on consistency, not intensity: It's easy to get caught up in doing things perfectly and intensely, but consistency is what truly leads to progress. Instead of expecting to do everything at once or perfectly, focus on consistent, steady effort. Small, daily actions will compound over time, bringing you closer to your goals.

Let go of the fear of imperfection: Perfectionism is often driven by fear—fear of judgment, failure, or not being good enough. Let go of the fear that holds you back from taking action or trying new things. When you focus on progress, you free yourself from the fear of imperfection and embrace the freedom to grow, learn, and evolve.

Affirmations for embracing progress, not perfection:

I am committed to making progress, not achieving perfection.

Every step I take is a step toward growth and improvement.

I learn from my mistakes and use them as opportunities to grow.

I celebrate the small wins along the way.

I release the need to be perfect and embrace the beauty of the journey.

Progress is more important than perfection, and I honor my growth.

I trust the process and am patient with myself.

I am proud of the progress I've made and excited for the progress ahead.

I focus on consistency and effort, not flawless execution.

I embrace imperfection as a natural part of the learning process.

Prompt: Be thankful for the opportunity to make progress.

Perfection may be a distant ideal, but progress is real and achievable. Every small effort you make, every step you take, brings you closer to becoming the person you are meant to be. Be thankful for the progress you've made so far and for the growth that is yet to come. Your journey is unfolding beautifully, one step at a time.

Example:

I'm thankful for the progress I've made, no matter how small it may seem. Every day, I take steps toward becoming the person I want to be. I embrace the process of learning and growing, knowing that perfection is not the goal. I am proud of the progress I've achieved, and I look forward to the progress I will continue to make.

TWELVE

Connect to Your Inner Child

Within each of us lies an inner child—the part of us that is playful, curious, imaginative, and full of wonder. Our inner child represents the purest essence of who we are, before the world's expectations, fears, and limitations shaped us. It's the part of ourselves that knows how to dream big, laugh freely, and experience joy in the simplest of moments. Connecting to your inner child is about reawakening that playful, creative energy that's always been within you and letting it guide you toward a more joyful, authentic, and fulfilling life.

As adults, it's easy to forget the importance of this connection. We become so focused on responsibilities, goals, and expectations that we lose touch with the part of us that simply wants to be happy and free. But when we reconnect with our inner child, we tap into a wellspring of creativity, joy, and a sense of wonder that can bring a fresh perspective to our lives.

Here's how to connect with your inner child:

Revisit your childhood passions: Think back to the activities you loved as a child. What brought you joy and made you feel alive? Whether it was drawing, playing sports, singing, dancing, or spending time outdoors, make time for these activities in your adult life. Reconnect with the hobbies or interests that once sparked your creativity and passion. Even if you haven't done them in years, revisiting them can reignite that playful, carefree energy.

Embrace curiosity and wonder: Children have an innate sense of curiosity—they ask endless questions and are fascinated by the world around them. Reconnect with your inner child by approaching life with curiosity. Explore new interests, ask questions, and allow yourself to wonder without needing all the answers. Let go of any cynicism or judgments and rediscover the magic in the world.

Practice playfulness: Play isn't just for children—it's for adults too! Play is an essential part of life that brings joy, creativity, and relaxation. Make time to play, whether it's through games, creative projects, spontaneous dancing, or laughing with friends. Allow yourself to have fun without worrying about productivity or perfection. Playfulness helps you reconnect with the joy of being present in the moment.

Release the need for perfection: Children are free from the pressures of perfectionism—they make mistakes, fall down, and keep going without self-judgment. Reconnect with your inner child by letting go of the need to be perfect. Embrace mistakes as opportunities for growth and learning. Give yourself permission to be imperfect, to explore without fear, and to enjoy the process of discovery.

Practice self-compassion and kindness: Your inner child deserves love, care, and nurturing. Treat yourself with the same kindness and compassion you would offer to a child. Be gentle with yourself when you make mistakes, and take time to care for your emotional needs. Reconnect with the playful, loving side of yourself and remind yourself that you are worthy of affection and self-love.

Engage in creative expression: Creativity is a natural outlet for your inner child. Whether it's painting, writing, crafting, or playing music, find ways to express yourself creatively. Don't worry about the outcome—just allow yourself to enjoy the process of creating. Creative expression helps you reconnect with your childlike energy and lets you express your emotions in a fun, unfiltered way.

Spontaneity and adventure: Children live in the moment, embracing the joy of spontaneity and adventure. Reconnect with your inner child by saying "yes" to new experiences and stepping out of your comfort zone. Go on an impromptu adventure, try something new, or say yes to opportunities that excite you. Let go of overthinking and allow yourself to experience life with a sense of excitement and possibility.

Laugh and be silly: Laughter is one of the most powerful ways to reconnect with your inner child. Let yourself be silly, make jokes, and find humor in everyday moments. Watch a funny movie, spend time with people who make you laugh, or just embrace the joy of being playful. Laughter is a natural way to release stress and reconnect with a sense of lightheartedness.

Spend time in nature: Children often have a deep connection to nature. They love playing outside, exploring, and being in the natural world. Reconnect with your inner child by spending time outdoors. Take a walk in the park, go for a hike, or simply sit outside and watch the clouds. Nature has a calming, rejuvenating effect that helps you reconnect with your authentic self.

Reflect on your childhood dreams: What were your dreams and aspirations as a child? What did you want to be when you grew up? Reconnect with your inner child by reflecting on those dreams. Even if they've changed over the years, your childhood dreams often hold valuable insights into what makes you truly happy. Revisit those dreams and see how they can guide your choices today.

Affirmations for connecting with your inner child:

I embrace the joy, creativity, and playfulness of my inner child.

I give myself permission to be curious and explore the world with wonder.

I nurture my inner child with love, care, and kindness.

I embrace spontaneity, adventure, and the thrill of new experiences.

I let go of perfection and enjoy the process of learning and growing.

I allow myself to express my creativity freely and without judgment.

I am deserving of play, laughter, and fun in my life.

I honor my childhood dreams and allow them to guide me today.

I treat myself with the love and compassion my inner child deserves.

I connect with the beauty of life through the eyes of my inner child.

Prompt: Be thankful for the wisdom of your inner child.

Your inner child holds the key to joy, creativity, and authenticity. By reconnecting with this playful, curious part of yourself, you unlock a deeper connection to your true essence. When you nurture and listen to your inner child, you rediscover the lightheartedness, imagination, and love that makes life richer and more fulfilling. Be thankful for your inner child, for it is the source of your most genuine happiness and creativity.

Example:

I'm grateful for the wisdom and energy of my inner child. By reconnecting with my playful, curious self, I invite joy, creativity, and wonder into my life. I embrace the lessons of my childhood and allow them to guide me as I move forward. I am thankful for the freedom and lightness my inner child brings, reminding me to live authentically and with love.

THIRTEEN

ACCEPT YOURSELF AS YOU ARE

In a world that often pressures us to change, improve, or be something we're not, true peace comes from the ability to accept ourselves as we are, in this very moment. Self-acceptance is about embracing who you are, flaws and all. It means recognizing your unique qualities, strengths, and weaknesses, and understanding that you are enough, just as you are. When you accept yourself fully, you stop striving to meet others' expectations or fit into molds that don't serve you, and instead, start living with authenticity and self-love.

Self-acceptance is not about complacency or giving up on growth. It's about loving yourself through every stage of your journey, knowing that who you are today is just as valuable as who you will become. It's about embracing your imperfections, understanding that they are part of your humanity, and realizing that they don't diminish your worth. When you accept yourself, you open the door to greater confidence, inner peace, and the freedom to live life on your own terms.

Here's how to accept yourself as you are:

Practice self-compassion: Self-acceptance begins with self-compassion—treating yourself with the same kindness, patience, and understanding you would offer a close friend. When you make mistakes or face challenges, instead of being harsh or critical, practice gentleness. Remind yourself that you are doing your best and that imperfection is a natural part of the human experience.

Stop comparing yourself to others: Comparison robs us of self-acceptance. It's easy to look at others and feel like we're falling short, but remember, everyone's journey is different. Focus on your own path, celebrate your unique qualities, and honor your own progress. You are not meant to be like anyone else—you are meant to be the best version of yourself.

Embrace your flaws and imperfections: No one is perfect, and your imperfections are part of what makes you uniquely you. Instead of striving for perfection, learn to embrace your flaws and see them as opportunities for growth. Accepting your imperfections allows you to release self-judgment and move forward with confidence, knowing that you are worthy regardless of your flaws.

Release the need for external validation: True self-acceptance comes from within. Stop seeking validation from others or relying on external approval to feel worthy. You are enough just as you are, and your value is not determined by how others see you. Cultivate the inner strength to validate yourself, trust your own judgment, and believe in your own worth.

Practice gratitude for yourself: One powerful way to cultivate self-acceptance is through gratitude. Take time to reflect on what you love about yourself, your strengths, and the things you appreciate about your life. The more you focus on what you love about yourself, the more you will embrace who you are and feel at peace with yourself.

Let go of perfectionism: Perfectionism often stems from a fear of not being good enough. By letting go of the need to be perfect, you allow yourself to be human, with all the beauty and imperfection that comes with it. Focus on progress and growth, not on an unattainable ideal. Celebrate the journey, not just the destination.

Honor your emotions: Accepting yourself means accepting your emotions, too. Allow yourself to feel what you feel without judgment. Whether you're feeling joy, sadness, frustration, or fear, recognize that all emotions are valid. When you honor your emotions, you create space for healing and growth, and you stop hiding parts of yourself in fear of judgment.

Let go of self-criticism: Often, we are our own harshest critics. Replace self-criticism with self-affirmation. Instead of focusing on what you think you lack, remind yourself of your strengths, achievements, and the qualities that make you uniquely valuable. Be kind to yourself, and speak to yourself the way you would speak to someone you deeply care about.

Embrace your uniqueness: Your individuality is your greatest gift. Embrace what makes you different and celebrate your unique qualities. Your experiences, perspective, and personality are what set you apart from others, and they are what make you special. Accepting your uniqueness allows you to live authentically, without the need to conform to anyone else's expectations.

Trust in your journey: Accepting yourself also means trusting that you are exactly where you need to be. Everyone's path is different, and there is no timeline for growth or success. Trust that every experience is part of your journey and that you are exactly where you need to be in this moment. Believe in the unfolding of your life and trust that you are always learning, evolving, and growing.

Affirmations for accepting yourself as you are:

I am enough, just as I am.

I accept myself fully, with love and compassion.

I embrace my flaws and imperfections as part of who I am.

I trust in my unique path and honor my journey.

I release the need for external validation and trust my own worth.

I am deserving of love, respect, and kindness, simply because I exist.

I let go of perfectionism and embrace progress.

I honor my emotions and allow myself to feel what I feel without judgment.

I celebrate my uniqueness and express myself authentically.

I trust that I am exactly where I need to be, and I accept my growth process.

Prompt: Be thankful for the gift of self-acceptance.

Self-acceptance is the foundation of inner peace and true happiness. When you embrace who you are, you create space for love, growth, and joy to flow freely. Be thankful for the ability to accept yourself fully, just as you are, and know that you are worthy of all the love and happiness life has to offer.

Example:

I'm grateful for the gift of self-acceptance. I honor myself as I am, with all my strengths and imperfections. I am worthy of love, kindness, and respect, and I give those things to myself freely. I celebrate my uniqueness and trust that I am exactly where I need to be on my journey. I am enough, and I am grateful for the peace that comes with accepting myself fully.

FOURTEEN
SOURCE OF HAPPINESS

Happiness is something we all seek, but it's often misunderstood. Many of us believe that happiness is something external—dependent on achievements, possessions, relationships, or circumstances. We think that once we reach a certain goal or attain what we desire, then we'll be happy. But the truth is, happiness is not something that can be found outside of us. It is an internal state that comes from within. The source of true happiness lies in how we choose to view ourselves, our lives, and the world around us.

Happiness is not a destination; it is a way of being, a state of mind, and an energy that we cultivate. It's not about always feeling joyful or cheerful, but about embracing the fullness of life—both the highs and the lows—with grace, acceptance, and peace. Happiness comes from within when we align with our true self, appreciate the present moment, and live authentically.

The source of happiness is not a single thing or person—it's a mindset, a choice, and an ongoing practice. It's about cultivating gratitude, nurturing meaningful connections, letting go of negativity, and finding joy in the simple, everyday moments. When we tap into this inner source, happiness flows naturally, regardless of external circumstances.

Here's how to tap into the source of your happiness:

Practice gratitude: One of the most powerful ways to invite happiness into your life is through gratitude. By focusing on what's going well and appreciating the good in your life, you shift your mindset from lack to abundance. Every day, take a moment to reflect on the things you are grateful for, no matter how small. Gratitude helps you find joy in the present moment and reminds you of all the blessings you already have.

Live in the present moment: Happiness thrives in the present. Often, we get caught up in regrets about the past or worries about the future, which prevent us from enjoying the here and now. By practicing mindfulness and focusing on the present moment, you can release stress, anxiety, and distractions. Embrace the present as a gift and find joy in the simple experiences of your daily life.

Cultivate self-love and self-acceptance: Happiness begins with self-love. When you love and accept yourself fully, you stop seeking external validation or approval to feel good about yourself. Instead, you recognize that your worth is inherent. Treat yourself with kindness, nurture your well-being, and celebrate who you are. Self-love fosters inner peace and joy that radiates outward.

Release the need for perfection: Perfection is an illusion that only leads to frustration and dissatisfaction. When you let go of the need to be perfect, you open yourself to the beauty of imperfection and the freedom to simply be. Embrace your flaws, make mistakes, and enjoy the journey. True happiness comes from embracing yourself as you are, not from striving for unattainable standards.

Nurture meaningful connections: Happiness is often found in the relationships we cultivate with others. Spending quality time with family, friends, and loved ones brings joy and a sense of belonging. Meaningful connections nourish our souls and remind us that we are not alone on this journey. Make time for those who lift you up, support you, and bring out the best in you.

Engage in activities that bring you joy: Happiness is often a result of doing things that bring you joy and fulfillment. Whether it's a hobby, creative pursuit, outdoor activity, or helping others, make time for things that nourish your spirit. These activities help you reconnect with what truly matters to you and bring you into alignment with your authentic self.

Let go of negativity: Negative thoughts, self-doubt, and criticism can block happiness and peace. Letting go of negativity is key to unlocking the source of happiness within you. Practice positive self-talk, challenge limiting beliefs, and focus on what you can control. Release old grudges, forgive yourself and others, and make room for joy to enter your life.

Focus on personal growth: Happiness is tied to a sense of progress and growth. When we are learning, evolving, and growing, we feel more fulfilled and alive. Set goals that inspire you, step outside your comfort zone, and embrace challenges as opportunities for self-improvement. Personal growth helps you tap into a deeper sense of purpose and fulfillment, which fuels your happiness.

Practice kindness and giving: True happiness is found in the act of giving. When you offer kindness, support, or love to others, you create a ripple effect of positivity. Acts of kindness not only make others happy, but they also make you feel good about yourself and your contribution to the world. Whether it's a simple gesture of kindness or a bigger act of service, giving back enriches your sense of joy and connection.

Embrace the flow of life: Life is full of ups and downs, and true happiness comes from accepting it all. Embrace the flow of life, knowing that both joy and hardship are part of the human experience. When you learn to navigate challenges with grace and gratitude, you build resilience and a deeper sense of inner peace. Happiness isn't about avoiding difficulty, but about learning to find peace within it.

Affirmations for connecting with the source of happiness:

Happiness is my natural state, and I choose to cultivate it every day.

I am grateful for the abundance in my life and the joy it brings.

I trust that happiness comes from within me, not from external sources.

I love and accept myself exactly as I am.

I let go of perfection and embrace the beauty of imperfection.

I nurture relationships that bring me joy, love, and support.

I find joy in the simple moments and embrace the present.

I choose positivity and release negativity from my life.

I am constantly growing, learning, and evolving, which brings me joy.

I spread kindness and love, knowing that it brings happiness to both myself and others.

Prompt: Be thankful for the source of your happiness.

Happiness is not a fleeting feeling that depends on circumstances—it is a state of being that you can choose to cultivate. The source of your happiness lies within you, in your mindset, your choices, and your ability to live authentically. Be thankful for the inner resources you have that allow you to create joy and fulfillment, regardless of what happens around you.

Example:

I am grateful for the source of happiness that resides within me. I recognize that happiness is not dependent on external things, but comes from my ability to embrace the present, love myself, and appreciate the beauty in everyday moments. I choose to nurture the happiness within me by practicing gratitude, kindness, and self-love. I am thankful for the inner peace and joy that I can create in my life, regardless of circumstances.

Thank You For Embracing These Concepts:

First and foremost, I want to extend my deepest gratitude to you for taking the time to explore these concepts and ideas. The journey toward living a more fulfilling, authentic, and joyful life begins with awareness, and I truly believe that by reflecting on and integrating these principles, you have taken a powerful step toward nurturing your well-being.

Self-growth is not always an easy path. It often requires us to confront our fears, shed old patterns of thinking, and challenge the beliefs that may have held us back for years. But this journey is also one of the most rewarding experiences you can embark on. As you've read through the concepts outlined in this book—whether it's learning to accept yourself as you are, connecting to your inner child, or discovering the true source of happiness—I hope you've felt a deep resonance with these messages. You are already enough. And your willingness to embrace these truths is proof of your inner strength and desire to live a more peaceful, authentic life.

The ideas shared in these pages are not quick fixes or one-time solutions. They are reminders to be gentle with yourself, to embrace life's ups and downs with grace, and to always choose to be the best version of yourself, even when life feels overwhelming. Remember, happiness is not something that is given to you—it is something you create through the way you think, feel, and act. Self-acceptance and self-love are practices, not destinations. The good news is that every small step you take toward cultivating these qualities adds up, and the effects are transformative over time.

We are all constantly evolving, and it is in the moments of challenge and uncertainty that we often find our greatest growth. Be patient with yourself as you continue this journey. Allow yourself to feel whatever emotions come up, and trust that you are exactly where you need to be. You are already whole, complete, and worthy of all the love, peace, and joy you seek.

In closing, I want to thank you for being open to these messages and for allowing them to guide you toward greater self-awareness and personal empowerment. The tools you've gained here are yours to keep and use whenever you need them. They are not limited to the pages of this book—they are available to you in every moment, every thought, and every choice. And as you continue to practice self-love, mindfulness, and gratitude, you will begin to witness more of the joy and peace that naturally arise from within.

Thank you for being a part of this journey. May you continue to grow, evolve, and shine brightly in all that you do.

With love and gratitude,
Paila Ravi Sankar

www.ingramcontent.com/pod-product-compliance
Lightning Source LLC
LaVergne TN
LVHW091236150826
845673LV00003B/1171